Affective

Jacob's Ladder

Reading Comprehension Program

Advanced Reading Curriculum for Social and Emotional Learning

Grade

3

Student Workbook Poetry and Biographies

Joyce VanTassel-Baska, Ed.D., &
Tamra Stambaugh, Ph.D.

Routledge
Taylor & Francis Group

NEW YORK AND LONDON

First published in 2020 by Prufrock Press Inc.

Published in 2021 by Routledge
605 Third Avenue, New York, NY 10017
2 Park Square, Milton Park, Abingdon, Oxon OX14 4RN

Routledge is an imprint of the Taylor & Francis Group, an informa business.

© 2020 by Taylor & Francis Group

ISBN: 9781646321858 (pbk)

Printed and bound by CPI Group (UK) Ltd, Croydon, CR0 4YY

Table of Contents

My Fancy

By Alexander Posey

Why do trees along the river
    Lean so far out o'er the tide?
Very wise men tell me why, but
    I am never satisfied;
And so I keep my fancy still,
    That trees lean out to save
The drowning from the clutches of
    The cold, remorseless wave.

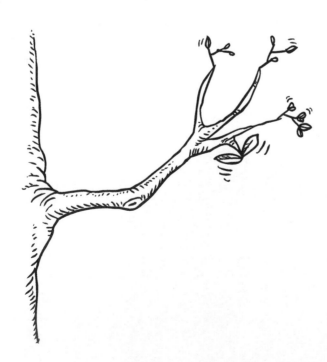

MY FANCY

Actualizing Potential to Advance a Goal

H3 Who we are early in life can determine what we become later in life. For example, Wilbur Wright played with toy airplanes daily from an early age of 3 and later with his brother discovered how humans might fly. Yet, often only beliefs and values and nonspecific interests carry over into adulthood. Lyndon B. Johnson loved people early on, especially those from his native hill country of Texas where he grew up poor. Never forgetting them, one of his first acts as a senator was to bring electricity to the hill country, an innovation that positively changed lives.

As a young student, what goals do you have to make the world a better place? What characteristics and/or experiences have shaped your desire to do good for others? What plans do you have to carry out your goals? Using a separate sheet of paper and other materials as needed, create a collage that represents your plan to date.

Understanding Roles and Affiliations

H2 1. How do your different roles and affiliations shape who you are? On a separate sheet of paper, draw a circle and put an image of yourself in the center. Then, draw four smaller circles that connect to you and label them: (1) student, (2) son or daughter, (3) friend, (4) neighbor.

2. Use descriptive phrases to depict your behavior when you interact with members of each of your subcircles (try to identify three).

3. Now analyze similarities and differences among your ways of responding to the different roles you assume. What does it reveal about your personality, your values, or your beliefs?

Role Assumed	Behavior in the Role	Traits Revealed

4. Using a separate sheet of paper and other materials as needed, make a large cartoon figure of yourself and label it with descriptions that you feel are most appropriate to describe yourself, based on this exercise.

Knowing Oneself

H1 What is the poet's fancy? Make a list of the characteristics he reveals about himself in his explanation of the reasons behind the leaning of the tree. Then identify the source of such a characteristic.

Characteristics Revealed	Source of His Characteristics

The Fly

By William Blake

Little fly,
Thy summer's play
My thoughtless hand
Has brushed away.

Am not I
A fly like thee?
Or art not thou
A man like me?

For I dance
And drink and sing,
Till some blind hand
Shall brush my wing.

If thought is life
And strength and breath,
And the want
Of thought is death,

Then am I
A happy fly,
If I live,
Or if I die.

THE FLY

Using Emotion

E3 How do both the poem and the drawing reveal how Blake feels about "man"? How do they both treat the concept of thinking? Using a separate sheet of paper and other materials as needed, create your own visual of what matters most in a person. You may make a poster, a body with labels, or a picture to convey your thoughts.

Expressing Emotion

E2 Write a short monologue about what you think the man is thinking and feeling. Share with your partners. Provide evidence from the picture to support your ideas.

_____

_____

_____

_____

_____

_____

_____

_____

_____

_____

_____

_____

_____

_____

_____

_____

Understanding Emotion

E1 Review the following picture, created by the author of the poem: https://en.wikipedia.org/wiki/Newton_(Blake).

What emotions does the picture of the man that Blake created cause in you? Make a list of what comes to mind.

_____

_____

_____

_____

_____

_____

_____

_____

THE FLY

Using Emotion

E3 Create a poem that features an animal or other creature in comparison to us. What emotions will you use to project the comparison? How do these words help convey emotions? How can you use words to convey emotions in your life through different ways?

_____

_____

_____

_____

_____

_____

_____

_____

_____

Expressing Emotion

E2   1.   What does the author mean by the phrase, "If thought is life / And strength and breath"? How is thought life? Do you agree? Why or why not?

_____

_____

_____

_____

_____

_____

_____

2. Make a mind map that represents your view of what life is.

Understanding Emotion

E1 The author identifies with the fly in the poem. What feelings does he cite that are similar? What activities? Make a list of both.

Feelings of the Fly and Man	Activities of the Fly and Man

Up-Hill

By Christina Rossetti

Does the road wind up-hill all the way?
    Yes, to the very end.
Will the day's journey take the whole long day?
    From morn to night, my friend.

But is there for the night a resting-place?
    A roof for when the slow dark hours begin.
May not the darkness hide it from my face?
    You cannot miss that inn.

Shall I meet other wayfarers at night?
    Those who have gone before.
Then must I knock, or call when just in sight?
    They will not keep you standing at that door.

Shall I find comfort, travel-sore and weak?
    Of labour you shall find the sum.
Will there be beds for me and all who seek?
    Yea, beds for all who come.

UP-HILL

Facing Adversity and Challenges

F3 1. What is adversity?

_____

_____

_____

_____

_____

_____

_____

_____

2. Choose your own metaphor to describe adversity. Create a poem, a picture, or a one-paragraph essay to explain the idea to your class.

Analyzing Adverse Situations and Conditions

F2   Name an "uphill" situation you have faced or are facing. How have you coped with it? How does the narrator of the poem suggest you cope with "going uphill"?

_____

_____

_____

_____

_____

_____

_____

_____

Recognizing Adversity and Challenge

F1   This poem has an interesting title. Why is it appropriate? Translate the first four lines of the poem into your own words and provide reasons for the poet choosing the title. What does the title help you understand about adversity?

_____

_____

_____

_____

_____

_____

_____

A Man may make a Remark

By Emily Dickinson

A Man may make a Remark -
In itself - a quiet thing
That may furnish the Fuse unto a Spark
In dormant nature - lain -

Let us divide - with skill –
Let us discourse - with care –
Powder exists in Charcoal –
Before it exists in Fire –

A MAN MAY MAKE A REMARK

Using Emotion

E3 1. Create a two-stanza poem of eight lines that describes in the first four lines an angry accusation, and in the last four lines the response to the accusation that "defuses" the anger.

_____

_____

_____

_____

_____

_____

_____

_____

2. Reflect: How does writing about emotions allow you to understand and control them? Write a few sentences in response.

_____

_____

_____

_____

_____

_____

_____

_____

_____

_____

_____

_____

_____

Expressing Emotion

E2 How can emotions gain control of our judgment, according to the poem? Give an example of an incident when this has happened to you (maybe in an interaction with a sibling, a parent, etc.)? How might you have handled the situation better?

_____

_____

_____

_____

_____

_____

_____

_____

_____

Understanding Emotion

E1 What kinds of remarks can people make that cause pain? That cause anger? That cause the need to respond? Make a list of at least three. How might you respond to such remarks in the spirit of Dickinson's warning "Let us discourse - with care"? Choose one from each column to respond.

Remarks That Cause Pain	Remarks That Cause Anger	Remarks That Cause Reaction

If the World Was Crazy

By Shel Silverstein

View the video for Shel Silverstein's poem "If the World Was Crazy" at https://www.youtube.com/watch?v=dNqZQriPSr4.

Listen to the poem twice, and then: (1) Identify key words and phrases that are highly descriptive and "create pictures in your minds." (2) Identify areas of life that Silverstein would change if the world were crazy.

IF THE WORLD WAS CRAZY

Actualizing Potential to Advance a Goal

H3 1. What aspects of Silverstein's poetry do you especially relate to? Comment on the following aspects:
- His use of language (provide an example)
- His visuals (provide an example)
- His use of humor (provide an example)
- His use of rhyme (first and third lines rhyme, second and fourth lines rhyme = abab rhyme scheme)

_____

_____

_____

_____

_____

_____

2. What do you see as Silverstein's strengths? Weaknesses? What words best describe his writing approach?

_____

_____

_____

_____

_____

_____

3. If you were to become a poet, what would be necessary for you to do?

_____

_____

_____

_____

_____

4. On a separate sheet of paper, create your own poem like Silverstein's that is also entitled "If the World Was Crazy." Be sure to create illustrations for each of the ideas you express in the poem.

Understanding Roles and Affiliations

H2 1. Review other Shel Silverstein poems (such as those here: https://www.harpercollins.com/blogs/harperkids/shel-silverstein-poems). Select five to read.

2. How does the poet get you to identify with the poem and/or its message?

_____

_____

_____

_____

_____

_____

_____

_____

Knowing Oneself

H1 Identify what you see as your strengths and weaknesses in a "crazy world" as a learner. Think of how you best absorbed the meaning of the poem.

Strengths	Weaknesses

Rosalind Franklin

Rosalind Franklin, a British chemist, was instrumental to the discovery of the structure of DNA. Her contributions to the discovery, however, are not widely known, nor is the controversy surrounding her work. Franklin was born on July 25, 1920, in London, England, to an affluent family. She was highly intelligent and knew by the age of 15 that she wanted to be a scientist. Her father did not support her pursuit of a scientific career, but her aunt and mother advocated for her to pursue her dream. Franklin was admitted to University of Cambridge in 1938, where she studied chemistry. After she graduated in 1941, World War II was underway. Franklin began working on her doctorate and was appointed as an assistant research officer at the British Coal Utilization Research Association. There, she studied how coal could be used most efficiently and effectively, which was highly relevant to wartime needs. She worked and researched there for 4 years, which resulted in her doctoral thesis and several scientific papers. She earned her doctorate from Cambridge in 1945.

After the war, Franklin moved to Paris, France, where she worked in a laboratory under crystallographer Jacques Mering. She learned, studied, and perfected X-ray diffraction, or using X-rays to develop images of crystalized solids. Following her position in Paris, she was offered a research scholarship in King's College in London. Her X-ray techniques were extremely valuable when it came to studying DNA fibers. When she started her position at King's College, little was known about the makeup of DNA. She and her graduate student Raymond Gosling were able to take photos of DNA and discover elements of its structure. One of their photos, Photo 51, became crucial to scientists' understanding of the structure of DNA.

During her time at the King's College lab, Franklin clashed with Maurice Wilkins, the assistant lab chief. The lab director miscommunicated to Franklin and Wilkins who would be responsible for leading the study of DNA fibers. Because of this, the two researchers never got along. He assumed she was supposed to assist his work, and she thought she was leading the study. Although they were both studying the same subject, Franklin and Wilkins worked completely separately, with Franklin having more success in the research. As Franklin made strides in her understanding of DNA, competing scientists at other research facilities were also working to understand DNA.

In early 1953, without her knowledge, Wilkins shared Franklin's Photo 51 with Francis Crick and James Watson, researchers at the University of Cambridge, who were working on a theoretical model of DNA. The photo confirmed their understanding of the 3-D structure and helix shape of DNA. With the knowledge from Franklin's photo, Crick and Watson were able to publish their findings. Crick and Watson received a Nobel Peace Prize in 1962 and were able to take most of the credit for DNA finding, even though much of their understanding of the DNA was from Franklin's photo. According to a footnote in the 1953 publication of their research in *Nature* magazine, they were "stimulated by a general knowledge" of Franklin's and Wilkins's work. Franklin and Wilkins both had articles in the same issue of *Nature* magazine, but it looked like their work just supported Crick and Watson's. It is likely that Franklin never knew Crick and Watson had based their findings on her research.

Because of her strained relationship with Wilkins and other issues at King's College, in 1953, Franklin left the college under the condition that she would not continue to study DNA. She moved to work at Birkbeck College in London, where she began studying the structure of the tobacco mosaic virus and the structure of RNA. She led her own research group and published 17 papers on viruses over the next 5 years. She completed much of her work while ill from cancer, continuing to work until several weeks before her death on April 16, 1958.

It is clear that, had Franklin lived, the Nobel prize committee ought to have awarded her a Nobel prize, too. Her conceptual understanding of the structure of the DNA molecule and its significance was on a par with that of Watson and Crick, while her crystallographic data were as good as, if not better, than those of Wilkins. The simple solution would have been to award Watson and Crick the prize for physiology or medicine, while Franklin and Wilkins received the prize for chemistry.

References

Biography.com Editors. (2019). *Rosalind Franklin biography*. https://www.biography.com/scientist/rosalind-franklin

DNA From the Beginning. (2002–2011). *Rosalind Franklin (1920–1958)*. http://www.dnaftb.org/19/bio-3.html

The Editors of Encyclopaedia Britannica. (2019). *Rosalind Franklin*. https://www.britannica.com/biography/Rosalind-Franklin

PBS. (1998). *Rosalind Franklin*. https://www.pbs.org/wgbh/aso/databank/entries/bofran.html

U.S. National Library of Medicine. (n.d.). *Rosalind Franklin: The Rosalind Franklin papers*. https://profiles.nlm.nih.gov/spotlight/kr/feature/biographical

ROSALIND FRANKLIN

Demonstrating High-Level Performance in a Given Area

L3 On a separate sheet of paper, develop a plan for pursuing your talent in the area you have stated as an interest. Identify goals and strategies for pursuing this talent. Identify resources that could assist you (people and materials). Present your plan to a small group and discuss the issues and problems you encountered in designing the plan.

Applying Learning to Practice

L2 Talent development for women has been a challenge in many areas. Science is one of those areas in which women traditionally have been a minority and undervalued. Franklin's difficulty in progressing as a scientist can be interpreted in many ways. Based on the biographical data provided, what might have been the reasons for (1) her not receiving official credit for her work on DNA and the resultant Nobel Peace Prize, and (2) her leaving King's College for Birkbeck College as her workplace?

_____

_____

_____

_____

_____

_____

_____

What steps might she have taken to receive more recognition for her work? Why does it matter?

_____

_____

_____

_____

_____

_____

Recognizing Internal and External Factors That Promote Talent Development

L1   Rosalind Franklin was sure she wanted to be a scientist from age 15. She had support from some family members but not her father. She was once quoted as saying, "Science and everyday life cannot and should not be separated." What interest do you have in science? How are you supported in that interest?

_____

_____

_____

_____

_____

_____

_____

_____

_____

_____

What strong interests do you have now? Who would be supportive of you in those interests? How might you learn more about related careers? Complete the chart outlining your thinking.

Interests	Support	Related Careers

Rosa Parks

Rosa Parks was a Black civil rights activist who, in 1955, was arrested for refusing to give her seat to a White passenger when a segregated bus became overcrowded. Her arrest sparked national outrage and was a pivotal moment in the Civil Rights Movement of the 1950s–1960s. Throughout her life, Parks faced numerous acts of racism and fought hard to dismantle racial segregation in America. Her efforts earned her many awards and honors, including the Presidential Medal of Freedom. She is noted as one of the most influential activists of the 20th century.

Born in Tuskegee, AL, in 1913, Parks faced racial discrimination from a very early age. She attended segregated schools until the age of 11, when she enrolled in a private school for girls. When her mother and grandmother both fell ill in 1929, Parks left the 11th grade to take care of them and did not earn her high school degree until 1933, a year after her marriage to Raymond Parks. Raymond was a member of the National Association for the Advancement of Colored People (NAACP), and he encouraged Rosa to join as well. She served as the youth leader for the Montgomery chapter of the NAACP from 1943–1957.

Parks became a well-known activist through her work with the NAACP, and by 1955 was thoroughly involved in advocating for social justice. When she boarded a segregated bus in Montgomery in 1955, she sat in the correct section as designated. But when the bus became too full and White passengers had to stand in the aisles, the bus driver told four Black passengers to give up their seats. Parks refused. She did so not because she was tired, but because she didn't think she should be forced to move just because of the color of her skin. Her refusal led to her being arrested and fined for violating the city's laws.

Parks was scheduled to appear in court on December 5, 1955. Her supporters, largely members of the Black community, helped organize a boycott of the Montgomery bus system to begin on that day. The boycott, led in part by Dr. Martin Luther King, Jr., used nonviolent forms of protest to stand up against racial discrimination. The movement, which came to be known as the Montgomery Bus Boycott, spread throughout the country. People in cities across the nation came together to fight segregation. The bus boycott lasted for more than a year and ended when the Supreme Court declared segregation on public

transportation systems to be unconstitutional. This small victory encouraged activists to continue fighting for their rights for years to come.

After that day in 1955, Parks was an advocate for change in the United States. She cofounded the Rosa and Raymond Parks Institute for Self-Development in 1987, in honor of her late husband. The organization provides support and resources to help young people reach their highest potential.

Parks passed away in 2005 at the age of 92. Her legacy continues to inspire social activists to fight for positive change.

References

American Academy of Achievement. (2019). *Rosa Parks: Pioneer of civil rights*. https://www.achievement.org/achiever/rosa-parks

Biography.com Editors. (2019). *Rosa Parks biography*. https://www.biography.com/activist/rosa-parks

Norwood, A. (2017). *Rosa Parks*. National Women's History Museum. https://www.womenshistory.org/education-resources/biographies/rosa-parks

ROSA PARKS

Demonstrating High-Level Performance in a Given Area

L3 Parks was a successful activist who created change. Using a separate sheet of paper and other materials as needed, create a poster to demonstrate your ideas about what success looks like for you. Include all elements that you think are important and design a graphic organizer to show connections among elements. Share with your class your graphic organizer and the reasons you have defined success in the way you have.

Applying Learning to Practice

L2 In what way was social and political activism a natural direction for Parks to take? What activities did she engage in to develop her abilities as a social activist?

_____

_____

_____

_____

_____

_____

_____

_____

_____

_____

_____

_____

_____

_____

_____

_____

Recognizing Internal and External Factors That Promote Talent Development

L1 What were the internal and external obstacles that Rosa Parks faced early in her life? How did she overcome them? Complete the chart below to show your thinking.

Type of Obstacle	Obstacle	Strategies for Overcoming	Evidence of Support (People, Experiences, Events)
Internal			
External			

Yayoi Kusama

Born in 1929, Yayoi Kusama grew up as the youngest of four children in a wealthy family in Masumoto, Japan. Her childhood was not a happy one. Her parents were the product of an unhappy marriage, with her father often absent from the home, ignoring his role as father to his children. Kusama perhaps suffered the most from this situation, as her mother used her to spy on her father, an act that left her permanently scarred emotionally.

At the age of 10, Kusama began experiencing vivid hallucinations in which flowers would speak to her and patterns in fabric would come to life and consume her. She began to draw these visions as a therapeutic outlet, providing her with solace and control over the anxiety that affected her. Her artistic talent was apparent at even a young age, and Kusama's work was shown in exhibitions all over Japan.

When Kusama was 13 years old, she was sent to work in a military factory sewing parachutes for Japan's World War II efforts. Her adolescent years were spent in the darkness of the factory, listening to sirens and the whir of planes flying overhead. The horrors of war would have a lasting effect on her, leading Kusama to create numerous antiwar artworks. Her factory job also provided her with the important ability to sew, which was useful when she began creating sewn sculptures later in her career.

Kusama's mother wanted her to simply be an obedient housewife. Kusama, however, chose to study art in Masumoto and Kyoto. The art training in Japan at the time used the ancient techniques and materials, used more than 1,000 years before. However, the stifling conservative Japanese culture and her abusive mother proved too much for Kusama, and in 1957 she moved to the United States, settling in New York City in 1958. She had come to intensely value individual and creative freedom. Once in the United States, Kusama was free to explore her artistic expression that was censored while living in Japan. She is quoted as saying, "For art like mine, [Japan] was too small, too servile, too feudalistic, and too scornful of women. My art needed a more unlimited freedom, and a wider world."

Kusama's artistic output during the next 15-year period was prolific and diverse, experimenting with various mediums such as drawing, painting, sculpture, performance, fashion, writing, and installation. She would sometimes work up to 50 hours without rest. She had the respect and friendship of

Reprinted from public domain.
https://en.wikipedia.org/wiki/Yayoi_Kusama#/media/File:Yayoi_Kusama_cropped_1_Yayoi_Kusama_201611.jpg

contemporary artists like Georgia O'Keefe, Donald Judd, and Joseph Cornell with whom she collaborated. Eventually the workload, coupled with a lack of financial security and Joseph Cornell's death, took its toll, and in 1973 she moved back to Japan to seek treatment for her mental exhaustion and declining physical health.

In 1993, she was invited to represent Japan at the 45th Venice Biennale. The acclaimed installation of one of her *Infinity Mirror Rooms* containing dotted pumpkins, coupled with the artist's performances alongside the exhibition, renewed the interest and appreciation for her work, along with the interest in the quirky artist herself. Kusama still seeks the limelight and continues to insist on being photographed with her work. In 2008 one of Kusama's *Infinity Nets* set new art auction price records for a living female artist and led to collaborations with luxury fashion retailers.

She is still organizing installations at leading museums across the country at age 91 to great acclaim. She never married.

References

artnet. (n.d.). *Yayoi Kusama*. http://www.artnet.com/artists/yayoi-kusama

Artsy. (n.d.). *Yayoi Kusama*. https://www.artsy.net/artist/yayoi-kusama

Tate Kids. (n.d.). *Who is Yayoi Kusama?* https://www.tate.org.uk/kids/explore/who-is/who-yayoi-kusama

WikiArt. (n.d.). *Yayoi Kusama*. https://www.wikiart.org/en/yayoi-kusama

YAYOI KUSAMA

Actualizing Potential to Advance a Goal

H3 Create a plan for yourself to reach a goal you wish to attain. What is the desired goal? What are the outcomes you want after the goal is attained? What strategies do you need to use to address the goal? How will you know you have achieved your goal? Complete the following chart to illustrate your plan.

Plan for Achieving Goal:		
Goal to Be Achieved:		
Outcomes Desired	**Strategies to Use**	**Assessment(s) for Judging Goal Attainment**

Reflect on the value of having a plan for goal attainment.

Understanding Roles and Affiliations

H2   1. What roles did Kusama play throughout her life? What was her role as a daughter? What was her role as an artist? A friend to fellow artists? How was art a pathway to self-understanding? Discuss these questions.

_____

_____

_____

_____

_____

2. Then, create a concept map that illustrates the impact of others and her environment on Kusama at different stages of her life (i.e., parents, education, travel, collaborators, friends, art itself).

3. Now rate the influences from 1–6. What do you think have been the most powerful affiliations in her life?

_____

_____

_____

_____

_____

Knowing Oneself

H1 1. Kusama only found herself and her art when she left Japan and then returned to the United States later in her life. Examine some of her art online, especially those created as three-dimensional experiences for viewers. Specifically, look at her Infinity Rooms and her Narcissus Gardens.

2. What does the art reveal about her as an artist and person?

   _____

   _____

   _____

   _____

   _____

3. Now read the short biography about Kusama.

4. Based on your understanding of Kusama, how did the following help her find out who she is: (a) education in one's area of interest, (b) travel outside one's own culture, and (c) collaboration with others?

   _____

   _____

   _____

   _____

   _____

   _____

   _____

   _____

   _____

   _____

Barack Obama

Barack Obama is best known for being the first African American to become President of the United States. He served as president for 8 years, from 2008–2016. His career before and during his presidency brought hope and change to communities across America, despite the hardships he faced.

Obama was born August 4, 1961, in Honolulu, HI. His parents met at the University of Hawaii in 1960 and got married soon after. When Obama was only 3 years old, his parents divorced, and he only saw his father one more time in his life. His mother remarried, and the family moved to Jakarta, Indonesia, where Obama continued to attend school. He returned to Hawaii in 1971 to live with his grandparents, with his mother also present for much of that time. Obama attended and graduated from an elite high school in Honolulu before going to Occidental College in Los Angeles for 2 years. In 1981, he transferred to Columbia University in New York City, and graduated 2 years later with a bachelor's degree in political science.

In 1985, Obama moved to Chicago, IL, to serve as a community organizer, but moved again in 1988 to Boston, MA, to attend Harvard University law school. There, he was the first African American to be president of the *Harvard Law Review*. In 1989, Obama worked as a summer associate at a law firm in Chicago, where he met Michelle Robinson. They married in 1992, once Obama finished his law degree.

In Chicago, Obama took an active part in registering tens of thousands of African Americans to vote through Project Vote. He was very involved in the Democratic Party and worked as a civil rights attorney while lecturing on constitutional law at the University of Chicago. In 1996, he was elected to the Illinois Senate, and worked to improve the lives of the citizens of Illinois. He helped improve campaign financing regulations, welfare and healthcare laws for low-income families, and criminal justice reform. Eight years later he was elected to the U.S. Senate and became well-known throughout the country after his speech at the Democratic National Convention of 2004. He spoke about his background and how all Americans are connected, regardless of their differences. This speech gained national attention and launched Obama into the

Reprinted from public domain.
https://en.wikipedia.org/wiki/Barack_Obama#/media/File:President_Barack_Obama.jpg

forefront of politics and the Democratic Party. He announced his candidacy for president in February 2007.

Obama became very popular due to his powerful speaking abilities and his promises to bring change to America. He gained particular attention from young and minority voters, and won the nomination over Senator Hillary Clinton. The race between the two was very close and historically important because no African American or woman had ever become president. Obama was criticized for being too young and inexperienced, so he selected Senator Joe Biden, who had been involved in politics for decades, to be his running mate. The team raised hundreds of millions of dollars from small donations and grassroots organizations, and gained enough support to win the election. On his inauguration day in January 2009, Obama became the first African American president of the United States. He received the Nobel Peace Prize in his first year in office.

References

Biography.com Editors. (2019). *Barack Obama biography*. https://www.biography.com/us-president/barack-obama

Brittanica.com. (2019). *Barack Obama*. https://www.britannica.com/biography/Barack-Obama

BARACK OBAMA

Reflecting on Patterns of Achievement

K3 1. What do you think were the three most impactful events that led to Obama's success in becoming president? Describe in a short statement how they fit together in positive ways for him to succeed.

_____

_____

_____

_____

_____

_____

_____

2. What events have been important for you in becoming successful as a student? As a member of a family? Describe in your own words.

_____

_____

_____

_____

_____

_____

_____

_____

_____

Assessing Strengths and Interests

K2 1. What strengths did Obama have? Using the provided biography, circle or highlight the strengths he possessed.

2. How can you use your strengths and interests to reach a goal? Write a sentence or two about how you can do this. Be prepared to share with others.

_____

_____

_____

_____

_____

_____

_____

_____

_____

_____

_____

Identifying Barriers to Achievement

K1 What do you think were the most challenging things Barack Obama had to face on his path to becoming president of the United States? Make a list of the top three and describe why they were barriers for him, and how he overcame them.

Barriers Encountered	Why Were They Barriers?	How Did He Overcome Them?